EARTHQUAKES

by Golriz Golkar

PEBBLE
a capstone imprint

Published by Pebble, an imprint of Capstone
1710 Roe Crest Drive, North Mankato, Minnesota 56003
capstonepub.com

Library of Congress Cataloging-in-Publication Data
Names: Golkar, Golriz, author.
Title: Earthquakes / by Golriz Golkar.
Description: North Mankato, Minnesota : Pebble, [2022] | Series: Wild earth science | Includes bibliographical references and index. | Audience: Ages 5-8 | Audience: Grades K-1 |
Summary: "The ground shakes. A road splits apart. Buildings collapse. It's an earthquake! Discover how movement deep below Earth's surface can cause such damage. Learn about earthquakes, what causes them, and how to stay safe during one"—Provided by publisher.
Identifiers: LCCN 2021042186 (print) | LCCN 2021042187 (ebook) |
  ISBN 9781663977021 (hardcover) | ISBN 9781666327151 (paperback) |
  ISBN 9781666327168 (pdf) | ISBN 9781666327182 (kindle edition)
Subjects: LCSH: Earthquakes—Juvenile literature.
Classification: LCC QE521.3 .G63 2022 (print) | LCC QE521.3 (ebook) |
DDC 551.22—dc23
LC record available at https://lccn.loc.gov/2021042186
LC ebook record available at https://lccn.loc.gov/2021042187

Editorial Credits
Editor: Ericka Smith; Designer: Tracy Davies; Media Researcher: Svetlana Zhurkin; Production Specialist: Katy LaVigne

Image Credits
Getty Images: Daniel Berehulak, 29, ImaZinS/Plan Shoot, 28, Stocktrek Images, 17; Shutterstock: Ahmet Ayunal, 12, Alex Millauer, 26, Angel McNall Photography, 5, austinding, cover, 3, Belish, 19, BlueRingMedia, 15, bogadeva1983, 11, Designua, 21, dynamic (map background), back cover and throughout, Everett Collection, 22, Frans Delian, 23, Kolonko, 4, Kurniawan Rizqi, 14, Marisa Estivill, 13, pashabo, cover (logo), Raftel, 24, Roger Brown Photography, 27, VectorMine, 7, View Apart, 9; USGS: 1, 25

All internet sites appearing in back matter were available and accurate when this book was sent to press.

TABLE OF CONTENTS

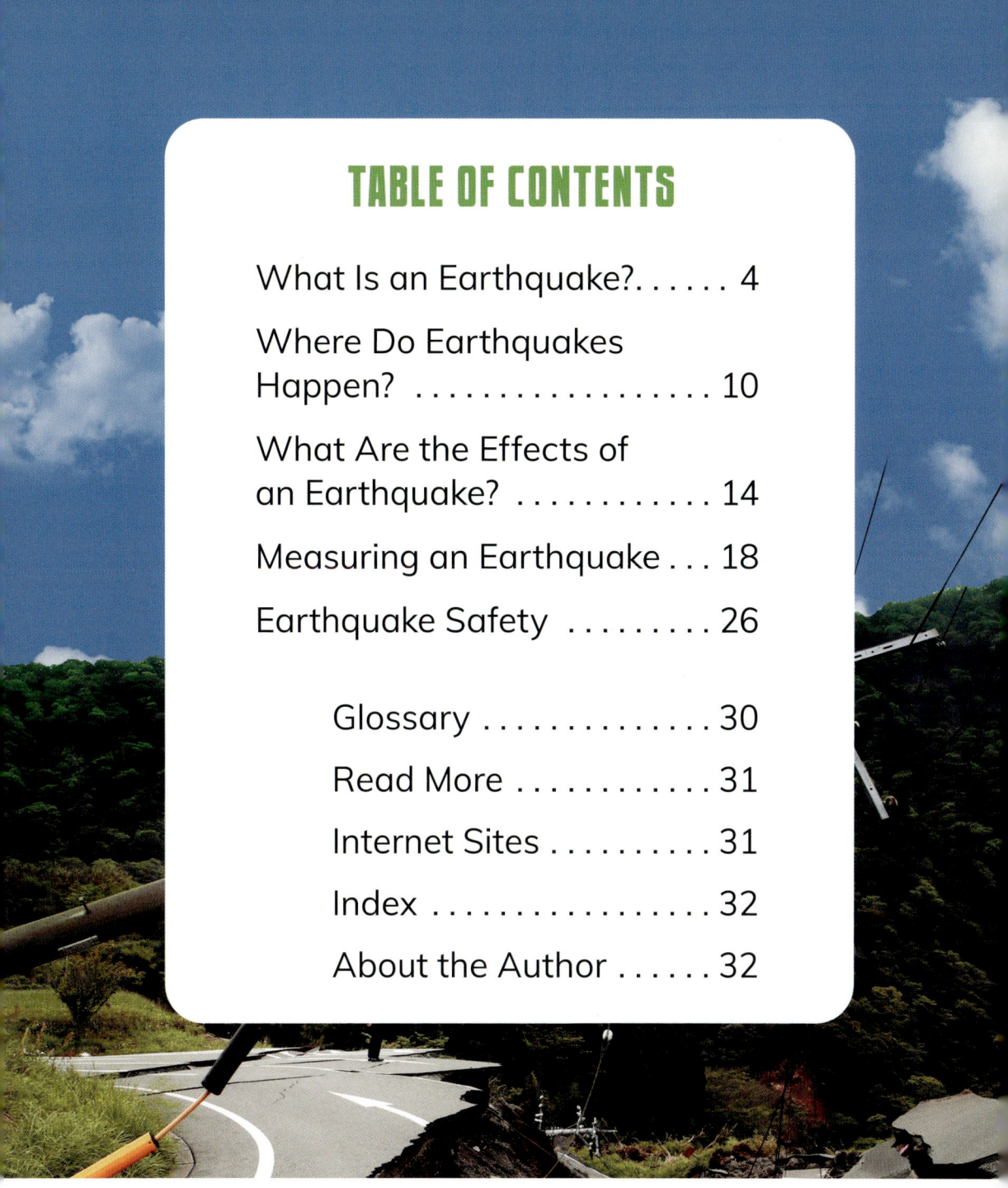

Words in **bold** are in the glossary.

WHAT IS AN EARTHQUAKE?

Earth's surface looks like one piece of land. But it's more like a puzzle! Earth's surface is called the **crust**. It is made of giant rocks. Those rocks are called **plates**.

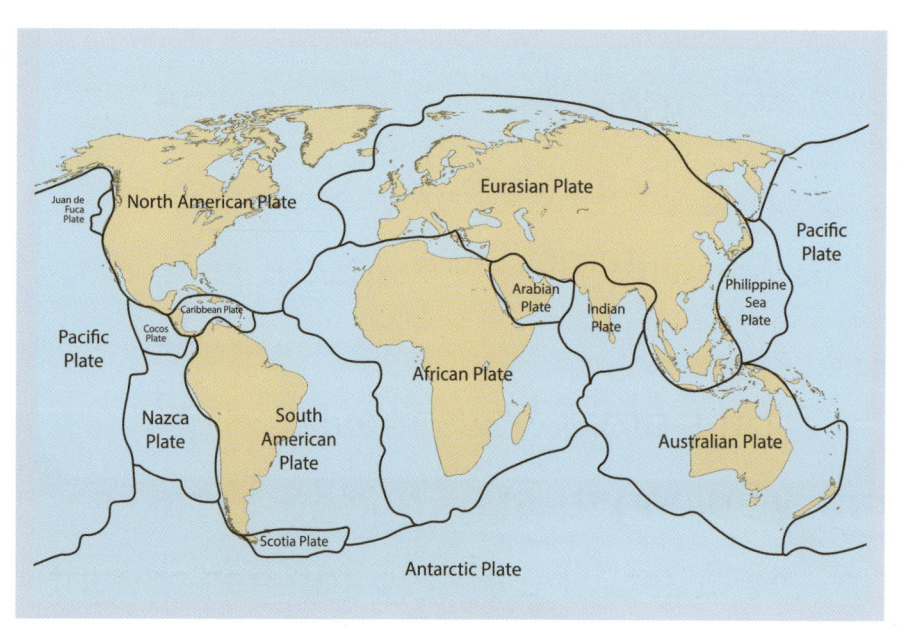

Earth's crust has a few large plates and several small ones.

The San Andreas Fault in California

Plates are always moving. They move along **faults**. Faults are cracks in the crust. The plates can get caught on each other. This creates **friction**.

Over time, **pressure** builds. It becomes too great. Then, the plates shift. This releases the pressure. It creates vibrations. They spread through the rock. The earth shakes. It's an earthquake!

An earthquake begins below ground. This is called the **focus**. On the surface, the spot above where it starts is the **epicenter**. The strongest vibrations are felt here.

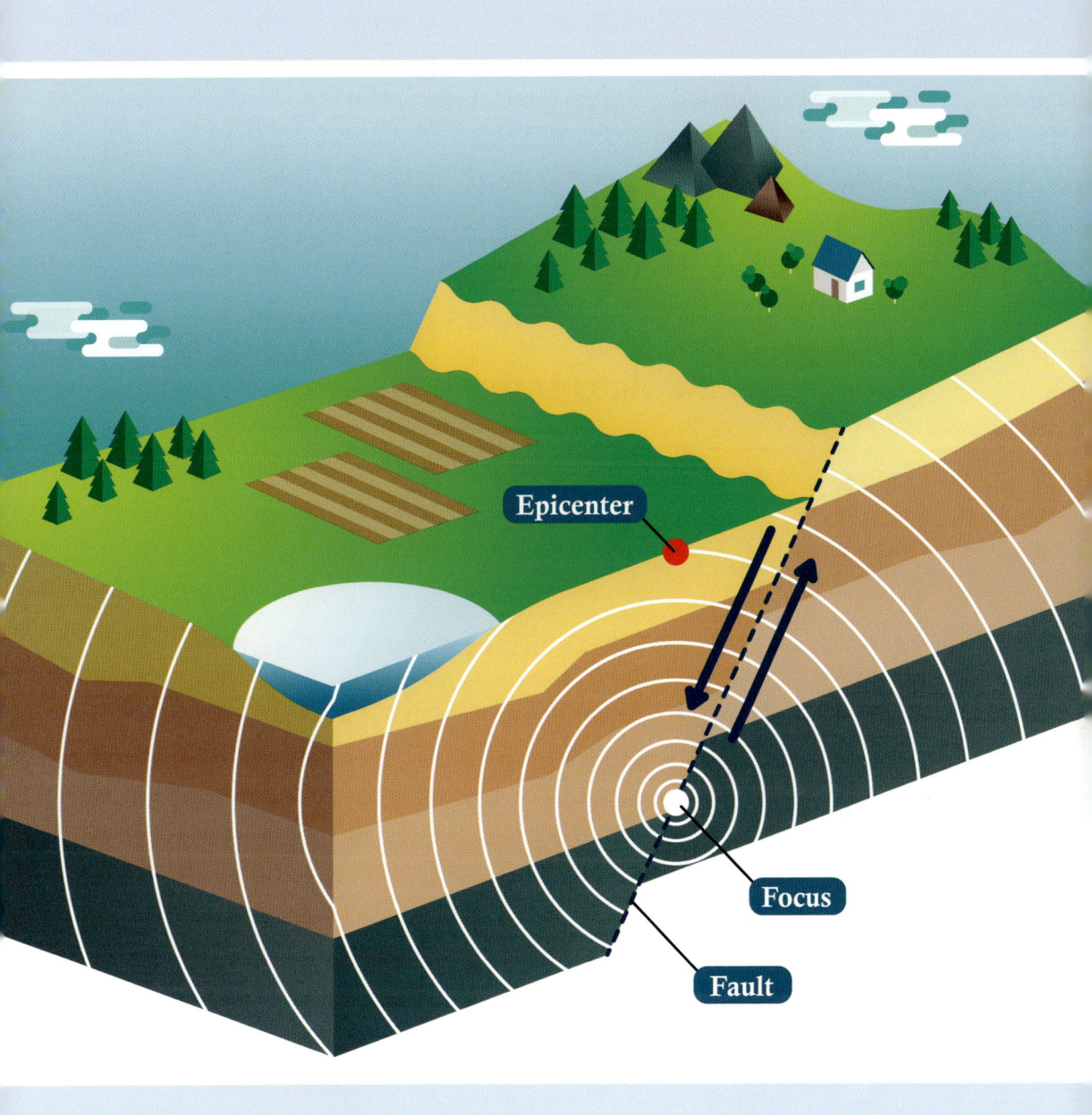

Epicenter

Focus

Fault

Earthquakes happen under the oceans too. The seafloor may shake. It may break apart. **Landslides** might happen. These landslides can cause giant waves called **tsunamis**.

Thousands of earthquakes happen every year. They happen all over the world. Most are small. They are deep in the ground. People usually do not feel them. Some are big. People near and far feel them.

Southern California has many earthquakes each year. Most are too weak for people to feel.

WHERE DO EARTHQUAKES HAPPEN?

Most earthquakes begin near the faults where plates meet. Areas with large faults are called belts. There are three belts where most earthquakes occur.

The biggest is called the Ring of Fire. It surrounds the Pacific Ocean. Volcanoes line this belt. The area is very active. As much as 90 percent of earthquakes start there.

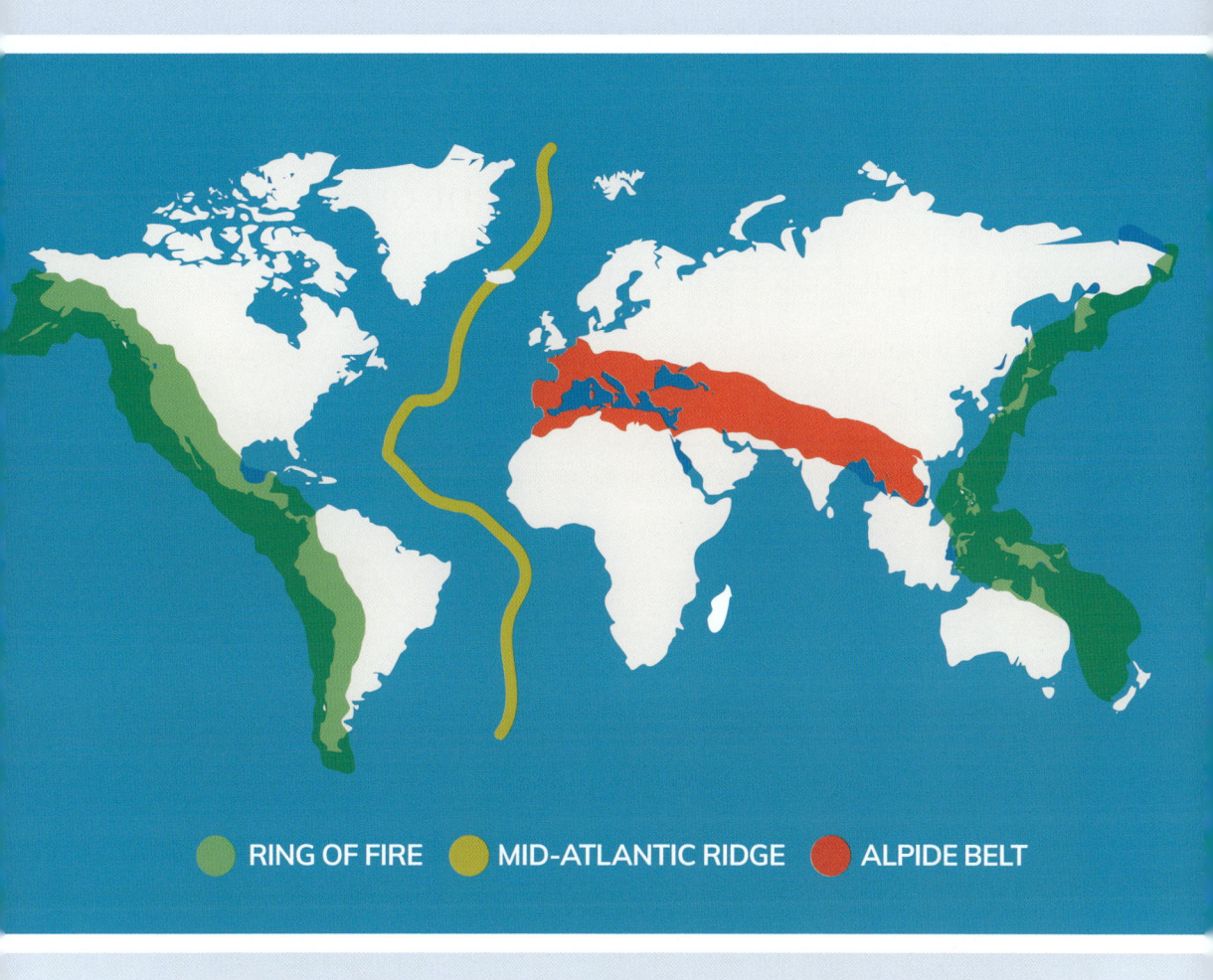

RING OF FIRE   MID-ATLANTIC RIDGE   ALPIDE BELT

Most earthquakes happen along the Ring of Fire
and the Alpide Belt.

The second is the Alpide Belt. It starts in the Mediterranean region. It runs through Asia and meets the Ring of Fire. About 5 percent of earthquakes start there.

In 2020, an earthquake hit Turkey, which is in the Alpide Belt.

Part of the third belt runs through Iceland.

The third belt runs through much of the Atlantic Ocean. It starts just south of the North Pole. It ends just north of Antarctica. This belt is mostly underwater.

WHAT ARE THE EFFECTS OF AN EARTHQUAKE?

Small earthquakes usually do not cause harm. Large earthquakes do. They damage buildings. Roads may break apart. Bridges may fall. Landslides and **avalanches** may also follow.

A bridge that fell after an earthquake and a tsunami

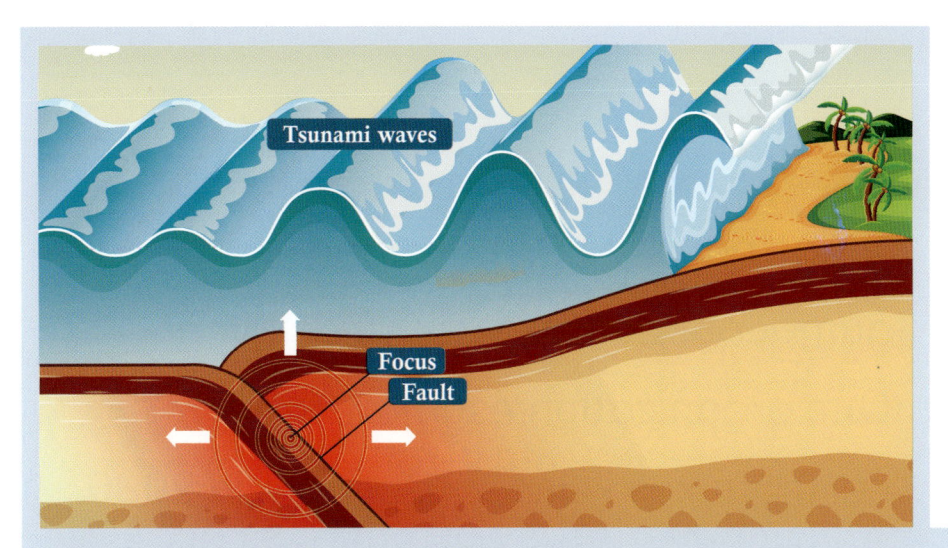

An underwater earthquake pushes waves of water toward land.

Large earthquakes may have **aftershocks**. These are smaller earthquakes. They happen after the main earthquake. They happen as the crust settles. New faults may form.

Underwater earthquakes can also affect land. They cause tsunamis. The waves come ashore. They flood the land.

Earthquakes can be deadly. The number of deaths varies each year. One organization estimates that earthquakes killed 231 people in 2000. It estimates they caused more than 226,000 deaths in 2010. That year a big earthquake hit Haiti. It caused many of those deaths.

Large earthquakes can cause a lot of damage too. In 1964, an earthquake hit Alaska. It caused $311 million worth of damage.

In 2010, a strong earthquake in Haiti killed many people and caused a lot of damage.

MEASURING AN EARTHQUAKE

Earthquakes can't be measured above ground. Faults are deep in the ground. So earthquakes are measured below the surface. Scientists use a machine to do this. It measures the vibrations. The measurements tell us the earthquake's **magnitude**.

This machine records the size of an earthquake's vibrations.

Scientists use several scales for measuring magnitude. One scale is the moment magnitude scale. It measures strong earthquakes well.

Another is the Richter scale. People usually don't feel an earthquake that measures less than a 3 on the Richter scale.

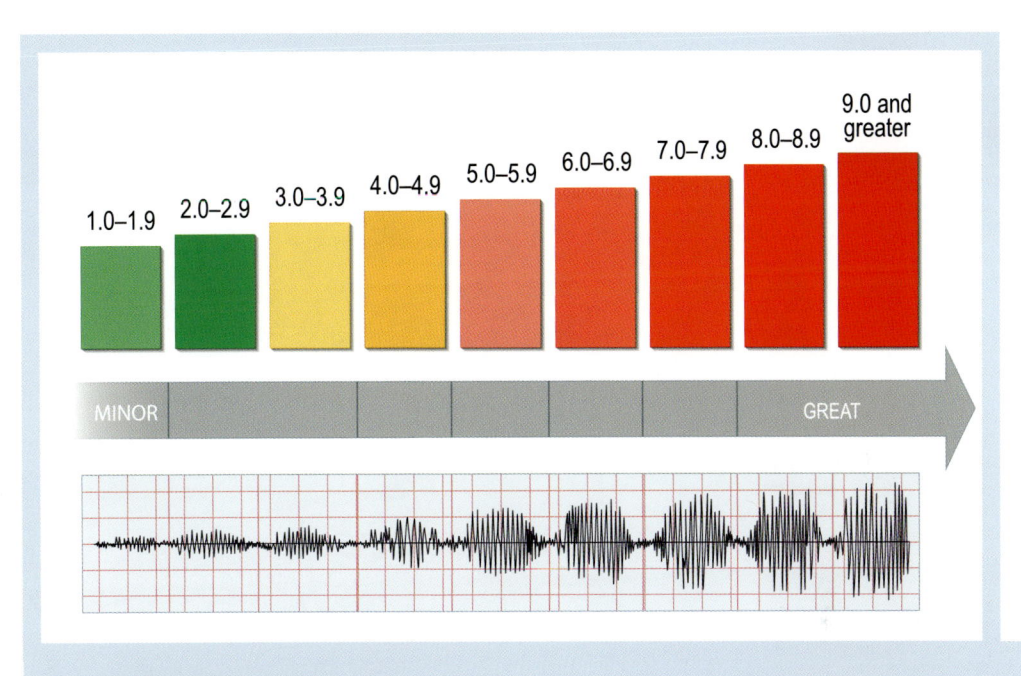

The Richter scale

Earthquakes between 3 and 5 are small. Some might cause damage. An earthquake between 5 and 7 will cause damage. And an earthquake between 7 and 8 can cause serious damage. Earthquakes higher than 8 cause lots of damage.

Damage from the earthquake that hit
San Francisco, California, in 1906

In 1906, a large earthquake rocked
San Francisco. It measured 7.9 on the
Richter scale. It destroyed most of
the city. It caused about $400 million
in damage. Some scientists estimate it
killed about 3,000 people.

In 2004, a 9.1 earthquake hit the Indian Ocean. It caused a tsunami. The giant waves hit areas in Asia and Africa. It caused $10 million in damage. More than 230,000 people died.

Damage in Indonesia from a 2004 earthquake and tsunami

An earthquake's intensity describes the strength of the shaking. The intensity can change. It might be stronger in one place than in another. Usually, it is strongest near an earthquake's epicenter.

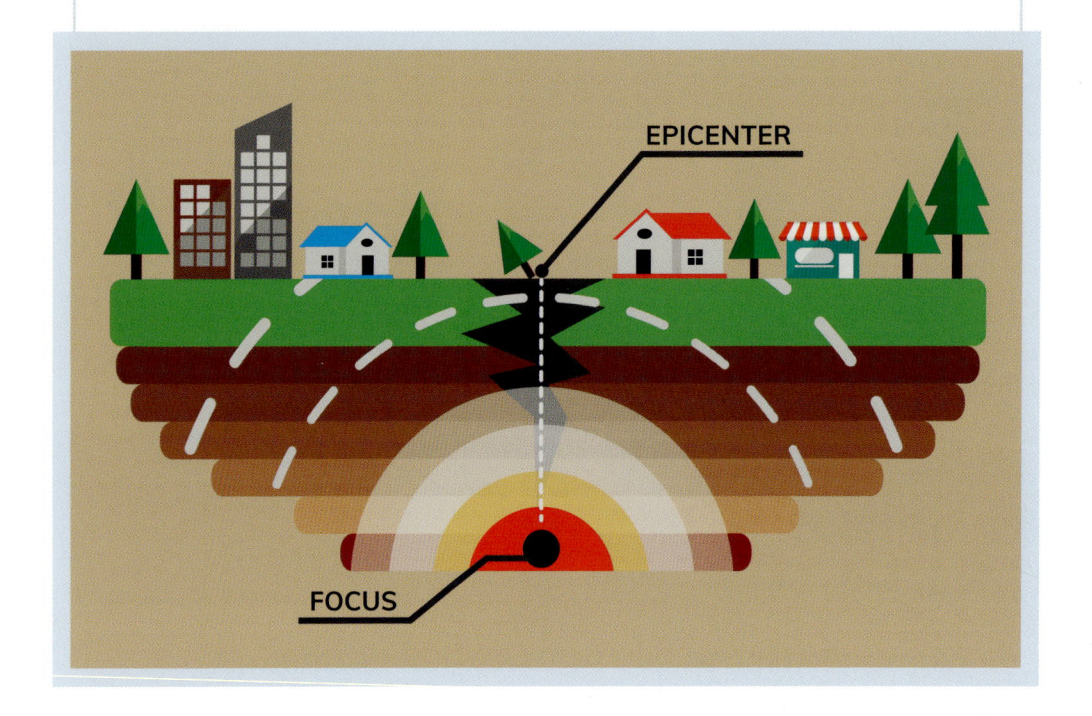

Damage to a highway near the epicenter of an earthquake that hit California in 1994

EARTHQUAKE SAFETY

Scientists cannot predict earthquakes. They guess where earthquakes might happen. Earthquakes can happen anywhere. But areas near major fault lines are earthquake zones. People in these areas prepare ahead of time. This helps keep them safe.

Your family can prepare too. Attach heavy furniture to walls. This stops it from tipping over. Pack an emergency kit. Keep the kit at home or in the car. It should include:

- food
- water
- first aid supplies
- clothes
- blanket
- radio

Here are some ways to stay safe during an earthquake:

- If you are inside, get under a heavy table.
- If you are outside, stay away from buildings. Open areas are safest.
- If you are near a beach, move away from the shore.
- If you are in a car, stay inside the vehicle.
- If you are not home, return home only when it is safe.

Earthquakes are natural events. They happen all the time. Many are too small to feel. Being prepared can help keep you safe when big earthquakes do happen.

GLOSSARY

aftershock (AF-tur-shok)—a smaller earthquake that follows a big earthquake

avalanche (A-vuh-lanch)—a mass of snow, rocks, ice, or soil that slides down a mountain slope

crust (KRUHST)—the thin outer layer of the earth's surface

epicenter (EP-ih-sen-ter)—the point on the earth's surface directly above the place where an earthquake occurs

fault (FAWLT)—a crack in the earth where two plates meet

focus (FOH-kuhs)—the point in a fault where an earthquake begins

friction (FRIK-shuhn)—a force produced when two objects rub against each other; friction slows down objects

landslide (LAND-slide)—a large amount of earth and rocks that suddenly slides down a slanted area

magnitude (MAG-nuh-tood)—a measure of the amount of energy released by an earthquake

plate (PLAYT)—a large sheet of rock that is a piece of the earth's crust

pressure (PRESH-ur)—the force produced by pressing on something

tsunami (soo-NAH-mee)—large, destructive waves caused by an underwater earthquake or volcano

READ MORE

Baker, John R. *The World's Worst Earthquakes*. North Mankato, MN: Capston, 2017.

Jacobs, Robin. *Earth-Shattering Events: Volcanoes, Earthquakes, Cyclones, Tsunamis, and Other Natural Disasters*. London: Cicada Books, 2020.

Prager, Ellen J. *Jump Into Science: Earthquakes*. Washington, D.C.: National Geographic Kids, 2017.

INTERNET SITES

BBC Bitesize: "Earthquakes"
bbc.co.uk/bitesize/topics/z849q6f/articles/zj89t39

Nasa Science Space Place: "What Is an Earthquake?"
spaceplace.nasa.gov/earthquakes/en/

National Geographic Kids: "Earthquake"
kids.nationalgeographic.com/science/article/earthquake

INDEX

ABOUT THE AUTHOR

Golriz Golkar is the author of more than 40 nonfiction books for children. Inspired by her work as an elementary school teacher, she loves to write the kinds of books that students are excited to read. Golriz holds a B.A. in American literature and culture from UCLA and an Ed.M. in language and literacy from Harvard. She loves to travel and study languages. Golriz lives in France with her husband and young daughter, Ariane.